A collection of my thoughts on the BDSM lifestyle.

Copyright © 2017 by Frank Corso

For information contact; fpcorso@outlook.com

Contents

Introduction

In the Tampa Bay area, I am known as Master Paul. I started my journey in BDSM in 1982 at a club in New York City. I was trained to be a Master from the bottom up. Meaning I started out as a submissive training to be a Master. I always stayed anonymous until I married in 1997. I became active in the Florida and Tampa Bay area community. A nickname my ex-wife had given me about 5 years before. I had founded a munch and I was considered a community leader. Just because of my munch and the parties I would host. What is a munch? It is a gathering of folks that are into the BDSM lifestyle at a vanilla restaurant to meet and fellowship. There all over the place here in Florida.

Nicknames are common in BDSM I learned that early on. Times have changed for BDSM it is more accepted then it was when I started. The club I attended in 1982 required hoops today clubs just require an ID. Support groups are more common today. In 2002, I attempted to start a support group called M.A.s.T which stands for Masters And slaves Together. In 2012, I was successful in starting a group in Charleston West Virginia. In 1999 in my small Florida town I was successful in starting a munch. It had about 23 in attendance and ran through to 2001.

Today, there are websites that are built for social networking, not just pornographic pictures. There is lots of information and resources for people to learn. This book is a collection of my essays I've written over the years. Most are designed to help the submissive, slave and bottom avoid the many dangers that are involved in BDSM. BDSM isn't all that safe. It is full of predators, abusers and married people looking to cheat.

To Dominants, Masters, and switches

I know my writings are designed to help submissive/slaves but Dominant/Masters you should read them to and learn what not to do. Relationships take work. And I don't know how to warn you. Dominants should be trustworthy, honest, and caring. Dominants are not perfect. So, don't pretend to be perfect. Be good and protect the submissive. Don't cause harm. We should all be harmless. We need to show respect and not demand it in return. Dominants don't demand anything. Remember it is a power exchange. Don't take anything. But, allow it to flow. Dominant grow with your submissive. Don't sit back and make the submissive do all the work. Enjoy yourself. This should be fun for both you and your submissive. Make it fun.

Look forward to being with the submissive. Teach her/him. Don't force anything. Be good even when being sadistic. Earn trust don't be afraid to work for it.

Dominants the journey should be as a team. Respect the limits work within those limits. Don't be afraid to be you. Don't pretend to be something you are not. Keep learning. Don't be afraid to make mistakes. Own your mistakes learn from them. Dominant doesn't pretend to be perfect. No one is. Be considerate of feeling. Be mindful.

And one last bit of advice to thy own self-be true.

Oh, I need to add this, don't play games.

Essay 1 The different types of submissive

Sometimes we tend to speak in absolutes. We read a word like "submissive" or "dominant" and we forget there are different types of submissive and/or levels of submission. The type of submissive depends upon the person you are and how you choose to grow.

The Bottom:

In understanding the submissive a good place to start is "the bottom". The bottom is the person who in the BDSM lifestyle enjoys the pain. Wishes to be on the receiving end of the "flogger". The bottom may direct the session before or during the session, the bottom maintains the control. A Dominant can be a bottom and derive pleasure from the act of bottoming without submitting. The act of bottoming is not always sexual but most of the time it is. The bottom does not release real control to the top. It is more of a mutual partnership. Some good examples of "The Bottom" are those who are into the spanking sect of the lifestyle. I have met spankers who will tell you they are not submissive and they don't have a submissive bone in their body. They are in this for the sexual pleasure of the pain. The bottom is more of an act rather than a state of mind.

The bedroom submissive:

Next type of submissive is the bedroom submissive. The best way to portray this type of submissive is in every facet of life she/he may be like the bottom or a vanilla but when the bedroom door shuts the roles drop and he/she submits to the dominant. In the bedroom is where the power exchange happens. It is also where the power exchange stays. This is almost always sexual. In the bedroom, the act of submission is complete. However, when the bedroom door is open the bedroom submissive returns to the vanilla world or role.

The difference between the "bedroom submissive" and the "Bottom" is control. The Bottom is in control. However, the bedroom submissive gives control to the dominant but only in the bedroom.

The Psychological Submissive:

This act of submission happens in the mind of the submissive. It happens outside of the bedroom outside of the sexual arena. In his or her mind the submissive has a need to surrender to the dominant. The act of submission is a psychological event. She/he can give her/himself to the dominant. She/he can give as little or as much as the psychological submissive wishes or needs to give. Then she/he would become the responsibility of the dominant to determine her/his choices and directions. A psychological submissive can give up as much or as little as she/he needs to surrender. The surrendering of the power is the driving force. Once the psychological submissive surrenders she/he can, simply become nothing. She/he can abandon her/himself completely to her dominant. Trusting in the Dominant's strength. Thus, the power exchange is completed.

The Submissive with the slave heart:

This is the deepest level of submission. The submissive with the slave's heart wishes to completely surrender without becoming a slave. In the psychological submissive the submission comes from a psychological need to submit. However, the heart is a different matter. The love of the dominant is craved. The submissive with the slave's heart desires to give her/his heart as well as her/his submission to the Dominant. The psychological submissive needs are not in love to submit. However, I feel the submissive with the slave's heart has a need to give not only submission but also love with that submission. The submissive with the heart of a slave is at the threshold of completely surrendering her/himself to the Dominant. The level of trust is greater in the submissive with the slave's heart then the psychological submissive.

The Slave:

Unlike the submissive, the slave surrenders complete control to the Master/Mistress. Am I saying a slave has no limits? No, I believe we all have our limits whether those limits may be moral or cultural, I believe those limits do exist. I believe a good loving master/mistress will respect the limits of his property "the slave" and take care of the slave.

The slave has an undying need to become owned by her/his Master/Mistress. I use the think "The Slave" was an extension "The Submissive" but a few months back someone suggested they were two different creatures. And I wonder if that is true.

The Slave must feel completely owned by master/mistress. The slave feels like nothing until Master/Mistress gives the slave identity. When Master/Mistress is happy the slave is happy. Most of the true slaves I have talked to feel this way. They feel complete when with Master/Mistress. The slave beams when she/he brings Master/Mistress pleasure. The slave must surrender, and the slave is not happy until she/he has surrendered. The slave feels completed when surrendering to Master/Mistress

Whether you believe the slave is just an extension of submission or that the slave is a different creature all-together, the slave has the deepest need to be owned by master/mistress. The slave must also have the deepest level of trust in Master/Mistress

Final thought:

There are only 2 things that are absolute in life. Those 2 things are death and taxes. And some feel they can cheat the taxman. But if you know a way to cheat death please send me a private e-mail.

What I am saying is this. The above is just my take on submission. There are many different levels. But what is most important thing is that you must be true to yourself. The submissive is not better than the bottom and the slave is not better than the submissive. Remember the line from Hamlet "Above all else to thy ownself be true."

Essay 2 Consent

There is a foundation of the BDSM lifestyle that foundation is made up of different stones. Stones like trust and communication are necessary parts of any type of relationship.

However, above every this is consent. No one can force a person to be a submissive. We don't break people. We can't make them into something they are not, for example, making a submissive into a slave. However, some consider slavery the highest form of submission. Non-consensual slavery is against the law and immoral. Consent is the foundation of all we do. Before entering any M/s D's or BDSM or any other letters I may have overlooked, the person should know what they are becoming involved in or should have a basic idea. It is Dominants responsibility to see they understand what "Informed Consent" is. I know that is not a very popular view, however, this is not PC.

Why do I believe it is the top's responsibility? Simple this person wishing to surrender to you is now your responsibility. Whether he/she is submitting in the bedroom or her/his life they are trusting in you. Pain may come with your style of BDSM but harm should not. This is not a one-way thing (if someone says my way or the highway be smart to take the highway) and it is not 50/50 it should be 100/100. If you are a weekend player there is nothing wrong with that. However, if you are a weekend play be honest about it. Don't lead your submissive into thinking there is more. If you are the strictest Master/Mistress remember you are not god that slave should always know she can walk away. Never cross the line of consent. Never cause harm.

To the slave/submissive keep this in mind be honest. Know who and what you are getting into. Don't choose to walk into this blind then cry later because it was not what you wanted. If you call yourself a slave make sure the person you plan to call master knows what that means to you. Remember you never give up consent. Free will is what makes us human. You never lose that free will. You may surrender that will to a master and there is nothing wrong with that as long as that master knows and respects your limits. Yes, limits, we all have them and no matter how much you may yell you don't have limits the truth is the only one you are fooling is yourself. A major limitation is a death, and if you wish to die then my strong suggestion is to get help.

Consent tells the vanilla world, we are willing. But more important consent is a part of the everyday life. Without consent, we have abuse that is the bottom line. You can be full M/s or you can be the weekend kinkster, it doesn't matter if you are a slap & tickle or a hardcore edge player consent is the one thing that never goes away.

Essay 3 Is BDSM actually safe?

We all like to think we are safe in life but the truth is real life is not safe. From the big picture to the little events, life is a series of risks. Think about it we are born and protected in the cradle by mom and dad. Until one day we have to take our first risk. We stand. Then with standing comes the next in this chain of events we must walk. Those first steps can be frightening. Are you going to fall? Will you land on your bottom or your face? But no matter how many times we land on our ass, we walk. And we get the reward that comes with walking.

Then as we learn to walk the next risk will come "School"! The parent takes you by your little hand and drops you off to a room filled with strangers. The stage after stage we grow and mature then stage after stage comes greater risks. We think that a small belt will protect us in our 2-ton piece of metal with rubber wheels. Yet every day we strap ourselves in getting on a highway and take our death traps in excess of 55 miles an hour to get to our next safe place, the workplace. A lot of us like to think we are safe at work just like those in NYC on September 11, 2001. But the truth is danger can lurk anywhere at any time. Or we think our homes are safe until along comes Irene, Charlie, and Frances.

The truth is danger can come from anywhere. The truth is life is a risk.

Now think about this. We tie people up. We use floggers and whips. Is this really safe? "Oh, I'm D/s this doesn't apply." Really? Remember that if Master should take your house just because he can. That is D/s. Relationships are major risks.

We can take safety measures but that is not a guarantee of safety. However, the thing to remember is this "greater the risk greater the reward".

My first whip to learn was my 4-foot bullwhip. I did not learn on a person but I did learn with people. I was told as I learned the whip, this whip would kiss me in place I may not want to be kissed. I had a choice learn and take the kisses (the risk). Or walk away. I chose to suffer the kisses. I chose the risk. Today I have the reward a beautiful "Murphy single tail" and the shill to use it.

I laugh when some call BDSM safe. One miss hit with the flogger can damage a kidney, one miss placed knot and you will damage a wrist or ankle. Yet we call this safe?

So how safe are we really? We are as safe as we chose to be. We are as safe as the knowledge and skill of our partner.

Essay 4 Negotiation

This is an often overlooked part of BDSM, M/s D/s or top/bottom. But it is a very important part of the relationship. If someone won't negotiate then have anything to do with them. Abuser is that way and it is a major red flag. It is the right of every slave, submissive and bottom to negotiate. Let no one tell you it isn't.

How to negotiate is simple. Make a list of your limits. Yes, you are allowed to have limits. Whether you are a slave, bottom or submissive you have a right to limits. If someone tells you, you aren't allowed to have limits have anything to do with them. A Master, Dominant or top should respect you and your limits.

After you make the list work together to see what you both want. Decide what you want to work on. Decide what is a soft limit and what is a hard limit. I personally believe hard limits should be off limits. But some don't feel that way. You must decide what you want to explore and what isn't open for negotiation.

Remember it is a power exchange. Meaning the submissive, slave or bottom has the power. If someone tells you different have nothing to do with them.

Final thought, I know how hard it can be to find a "good someone". But settling can cost you your life or worse a lifetime of abuse. It is ok to be picky. You should educate yourself and be aware of how dangerous this can be. When I first got into this back in 1982 no advised me and I got robbed. If you go by just looks you are asking for trouble.

Essay 5 Learning the single tail

A few years ago, I watched a man use a set of single tail whips. His precision was, as one would play a concert Violin. I watched as the two whips danced along the back and buttocks of the slave. I enjoyed the expression of rapture on the face of the slave as the whip master mixed pain and pleasure.

I thought to myself, I am a master of the crop and flogger how hard can this be? So, in my arrogance, I picked up a similar whip known as the 3-foot single tail. I snapped the whip in the air and I fell in love with the sound. I snapped it a second time watching the coil of the whip. Then like a snake, it recoiled striking back at me. It's target my testicular region. The bite was unbearable. I tossed the evil apparatus to the ground and walked away.

Since then, I have watched different masters work this "toy". My trainee Sir Jim's "d" wanted to experience it so I let her to one of these masters. I watch in awe as he made her body sing with both pain and pleasure. However, in the back of my mind, I would always remember the bite of that snake.

Then a few months ago I met inspiration and motivation. Her name was "slave Phoenix". I gave her the name. She awoke the dormant Master and the desire to learn & improve. This time I placed the single tail in my hand with respect, not arrogance. As I had watched, others do for years. Now my time had come.

I set up a self-disciplined training plan for myself. I took something and hung it. It was my leather vest. I know how much I love that vest so I know I would not damage it. To improve my aim, I took a pair of woman's thong style panties as a target. In addition, I practiced the whip with the respect knowing that one wrong flick of the wrist I would sing one octave higher.

This morning as I sit here sipping my morning coffee, I realize this single tale is the perfect metaphor for Dominance. When Dominance is used in arrogance, it will bite you in the balls. Being a Dominant should be a journey of self-respect, self-disciplined, inspiration and motivation and lastly the desire to learn & improve.

This was the lesson of the single tale.

Essay 6 Not an escape

To me, the lifestyle is not an escape from reality. To me, it enhances my life. I have been reading a lot of personal ads lately and some seem to be unable to either separate reality from fantasy. Or they are trying to escape life or some problem they might have. Fact is you can't run from your problems. You always bring them with you. The only way to get rid of your problems is to solve them. You solve them by working on them.

As to fantasy, I've lived most of my fantasies and I can tell you from personal experience real life is much more fun. That is coming from a real-time Master. I am a Master that was trained from the bottom up, a Master that owns his own slave. Fantasy can be fun don't get me wrong, but it gets old quick. Life should be better. For example, my coffee is ready for me each and every morning. Now my slave has issues so some mornings I should make it. Remember she is still human.

We are all human first with needs and I believe the Master is responsible to meet the needs of the slave. He, if he wishes, could grant the desires or wants of the slave. Those are not needs. But if your need is to run away from the life you need serious help. You can't run away from life. Life always has a way of catching up with you. If you have a need for control because you have no self-control again get help.

Essay 7 Levels of respect:

Before reading this re-watched the movies "The Godfather" & "The Godfather Part II" For those who don't know me this just a joke.

When we hear the word respect some things come to mind. For some, it is a song by Miss Franklyn. To others, it is something they think people should earn or they should earn it. To some, it was beaten into them while others have had it beaten out of them. It is a word that in the D/s lifestyle is beat (no pun intended) about a bit.

Level #1 basic respect or common courtesy:

Some folks equate common courtesy with respect. "Mind your manners boy or girl" is what most of us have heard growing up. A good example of this is you and your date enters a very nice restaurant, would you want your service from a respectful server or an ill-mannered person. Which is acceptable when we drive up to a drive-thru window, "Welcome to (insert name) May I take your order? Or ok what the "F" do you want? I wonder how many of would go straight to the manager and demand the head of such a disrespectful employee. This is a respect we demand but is it a respect we return? To the server in the fine restaurant you show it in your tip (this is enforced respect). And to the fast food worker, you show it in the smile and the polite thank you. That is common courtesy or basic respect. We should use basic respect in our daily lives. A smile to the postman or a polite thank you to the people in the 7/11 as we rush in to get the forgotten gallon of milk would be a good start. And if you ever want to feel real disrespect take a fast food job, it is hard work for the lowest wage allowed by law, with a stressed-out manager and customers who are in too much of a rush to show the smallest amount of respect.

Level one is the common courtesy we should show each other.

Level #2 enforced respect or the law & respect:

In level one (basic respect) there is no visible reprisal for the act of disrespect. There is no law requiring you to be respectful. You can growl at a server and you still may get the respect for the person and the fast food worker know if they are not nice it could cost them their job. But in level two it is not so the lack of respect for authority could cost you your freedom and in some case very quickly. If you think this, not true next time please feel free to tell the judge what you really think. Or please tell the state trooper you are not going to pay your speeding tickets or his hat is funny. Some of us pride ourselves on out impertinence. And there is a time and place for such insolence, but if you choose such a path you must also accept the fire you bring down on yourself. If you give the judge the finger then you may get free room and board for a short time.

I am a child of the 60's so I understand there are times for civil disobedience but this is not a dissertation on the subject of civil disobedience. I firmly believe in the right to protest. But I digress.

Level #3 earned respect:

I personally believe you should show the first level of respect even if you like someone or not. But that was the way I was raised. In my family, you did not show disrespect to my father's friends. But I digress. In this lifestyle, there are members that you respect them. And their respect is well earned. Then there are those of us that because of rumors or a relationship gone bad or just plain pissed off the wrong person have to prove we are people of honor. (I will not comment further).

But when it comes to this type of respect I have noticed those who earned the respect of the community did not try to. They just were themselves.

Last level Self-respect:

This to me is the most important level and without self-respect how can you respect some else. Because after all is said & done you have to face yourself in the mirror every morning and every night. There are a great number of reasons why a person would lose their self-respect. Drug & alcohol abuse is two of the two biggest killers of one's self-image. But also abuse also can cause your self-image to fade into the negative.

In my opinion, a good Dom will help to build the self-image of his submissive and not obliterate it. I am not talking about the approved humiliation that a submissive may enjoy. I'm talking about the abuse I suffered as a child & young adult. My own father would tell me that I was doomed to a life failure. I was 35 the first time I heard my father say, Son, I'm proud of you"

Self-image and self-respect go hand in hand. And I truly believe if you have no self-respect then you lack one of the basic keys to living and enjoying life.

Essay 8 Message to a new submissive/slave

So, you love service. And you have discovered the great world of BDSM. Allow me to tell you a few things. I'm going to tell you what I tell every new person whether they are Christian or not. You have to find what works for you. If you are happy being a submissive then learn to be the best sub possible.

First, find a Mentor. A good mentor is not a sexual partner. Mentorship is a personal developmental relationship in which a more experienced or more knowledgeable person helps to guide a less experienced or less knowledgeable person. However, true mentoring is more than just answering occasional questions or providing ad hoc help. It is about an ongoing relationship of learning, dialog, and challenge. * – Wikipedia, I suggest a good mentor would be another submissive or slave. Not that Dominants/Masters can't mentor a sub/slave, I do it all the time. But I just think someone who has been what you are going through would understand. I understand because I was trained from the bottom up. That means I started as a sub before earning my title of Master.

Join groups. Fellowship with other submissives is a good thing. You do not want to isolate yourself. Hanging and talking will help you understand what you are and that there are others like you.

Ask questions. Questioning is a good thing and a good way to stay safe. A Dominant/Master should be willing to answer the question. Ask other subs/slaves questions too

Also, just because someone claims to be a Master does not give them the right to start dominating you. If a Master that you have not negotiated with, tells you that you are a sub or slave, therefore; you have to follow their orders, then it is a good idea to cut off communication with them.

Don't settle for the first Master that comes along. Think of this as a romantic relationship. Do you marry the first man or woman that smiles at you? Get to know more than one. Until you are ready to make a commitment to a Dominant/Master/Mistress, you have the right to talk to several.

Also, remember that your feelings matter. In the play, a Dom/Master/Mistress might say that they do not, but this should only be in play. In r/l your thoughts, emotions, desires, and even your health matter.

Ok, let's talk about power and power exchange. And remember the submissive/slave has all the power. Not the Dominant/Master/Mistress, we have no power except what you give us. The power exchange can be a beautiful thing when done right.

The foundation and cornerstone of this lifestyle is consent. You have a right to consent. If someone does something to you that you do not consent to. Run away, don't walk, run. Part of consent is setting limits. You have a right to set limits. Submissive will do this within the relationship. A slave should set her limits in negotiation. Yes, slave, you have that right. You should always negotiate with a Master. If a Master says you do not have that right, run away.

Remember these: SCC & RACK. The first SCC stands for safe, sane, and consensual. A Dominant/ Master/Mistress should keep you safe and play safe. The use of drugs or alcohol during play is not safe because they alter perception and dangerous mistakes can be made.

Although what we do looks insane to the outside world, it can be very sane, and the bottom line is consent. Everything we do is with consent. You never lose the right to consent. Slaves, let me be very clear. You always have the right to walk away. If a Master tells you differently, he is not a Master but an abuser.

Next is what I believe and that is RACK. The R stands for risk. There is a risk in what we do. No matter whether it is BDSM, M/s, or D/s, there is a risk. Which brings us to the A. the A stands for aware. A Dominant/Master should make you aware of the risk you are taking. C=consent or Consensual, again I cannot stress this enough. It is the foundation and cornerstone of all we are. Last, the K is for kink. Yes, we are a very kinky people and remember your kink may not be someone else's kink. But that is OK.

Communication is essential. Keep in mind, a potential Dom/Master/Mistress cannot read your mind. If there is something that scares you or that you are uncomfortable with, tell them! If they are unwilling to listen and talk to you about it, run away!

Keep in mind that when a person is a Dom/Master/Mistress they are also human. They will make mistakes.

Respect should be earned I am not talking about common courtesy. Being polite always makes you look good. But respect is earned. And a Dominant/Master should never demand it. If a Dominant demand this you should run. We command respect by our actions. And a Dominant should be willing to earn that respect. One last thought on respect, you should respect yourself. Self-respect is important. If you can't respect yourself how can you respect someone else?

Trust is also earned. If someone is not willing to earn your trust, or if they demand your trust, walk away. You need to trust to have a good relationship. But trust needs to be earned. A dominant/Master should be willing to earn your trust

This is a great way of life or it can be. But it can be dangerous. It is used by abusers to abuse. It is used by pretenders and predators also. We wrote this to help keep you safe.

Essay 9 Personality Traits

Friendly

You would rather hang out with others than spend time alone, and you'd far rather be doing something with your friends than just sitting around. You're happy in a crowded room, club, stadium, or auditorium.

You're not a private person who is ill at ease in a group; you don't view excessive socializing as a waste of time.

Warm

You have a genuine interest in other people. You're a natural host and are always thinking about how you can increase the happiness of those around you. When friends have problems or are in trouble, you're usually the first person they turn to for aid and comfort. Scoring high on the "warm" trait suggests that you are among those who enjoy domestic activities — doing things around the house — and are enthusiastic about charitable work, helping others, and making the world a better place.

You don't always say exactly what you're thinking; you don't like the idea of causing anyone pain because of your criticism.

Understanding

You are willing to take the time to find out what's going on with other people, especially if they're in distress. You're a good listener, you don't criticize, and you offer unbiased, respectful, honest advice when it's requested. With a high score on the "understanding" trait, it is likely that you are enthusiastic about charitable work, helping others, and making the world a better place.

You don't feel the need to impose your standards on others or say things that, even though true, cause pain.

Scrupulous

You are an honest, fair person. You don't lie or cheat to get ahead. You treat others with respect and hope for the same in return.

You do not feel that you are above the rules that everyone else follows; you are definitely not willing to do whatever it takes to get ahead.

Empathetic

You are in touch with your own feelings, which helps put you in touch with the feelings of others.

You don't buy the logic that your happiness comes ahead of everyone else's because unless you're happy you're incapable of making anyone else happy.

Calm

You rarely become irritated, generally, accept people as they are, take things as they come, and feel relaxed in most situations.

You do not let a minor annoyance escalate to a confrontation. You don't regularly snap at those around you or fly off the handle with little provocation.

Passionate

You are in touch with your emotions, and sometimes you react before you think. The good news: you don't tamp down your feelings. The bad news: you sometimes say or do things that you later wish you could take back.

You do not live your life on an even keel; you do not go for long periods without experiencing some mood swings.

Intellectual

You are thoughtful, rational, and comfortable in the world of ideas. People find you interesting to talk to. You're the living embodiment of the saying "You learn something new every day." In general, those with a high score on the "intellectual" trait are employed in such fields as teaching and research and are enthusiastic about reading, foreign films, and classical music.

You do not avoid abstract conversation, experimenting with new ideas, or studying new things. It bores you to stick to the straight and narrow of what you already know.

Sympathetic

You have a knack for knowing what's going on in the hearts and minds of those around you, without their having to tell you explicitly. People tend to turn to you with their problems because they know you care, and that you will likely offer good advice and a helping hand.

You do not feel that people with sad stories are just looking for attention, or have brought their problems upon themselves.

Accessible

You're comfortable expressing yourself in words and actions, with no self-censorship. You believe that if someone doesn't like what they see it's not your problem, but theirs. A high score on the "accessible" trait suggests that you have a lot of friends, socialize often, and enjoy rap/hip-hop music.

You don't see the need to keep your thoughts to yourself or to have a zone of privacy that encompasses only yourself and a small circle of friends and relatives.

Essay 10 R.A.C.K.

What this means to me. And maybe what it should mean to you. This is not an S.S.C vs R.A.C.K rack conversation just my opinion of R.A.C.K.

R? Risk what is the risk to me? What is the risk to the bottom (Bottom Slave and submissive all the same for this conversation)?

This is always a risk in the BDSM activity. The risk might be small and risk might for big. For example, a whipping with a single tail, a single tail can break a bone or draw blood. And it can be used to kill. A simple flogging can have the same effect. If you strike in the wrong place you can cause damage. Rope Bondage can have risk too. You should be aware of those risks before engaging in any BDSM activity.

The same applies to a D/s or M/s relationships. All relationships have some risk. But I personally think the M/s or D/s relationships are riskier. An M/s or D/s relationship should not be 50/50 but a 100% both ways (Again my opinion).

A? Aware, both parties should be aware of the risk. You should educate yourself about your risk. Education is a foundation stone to building relationships or just play. Do you know what you're doing? How did you come to this knowledge? Did you attend a class? Did a mentor teach you? Or were you trained? When I went to learn the single tail, I took a class for a year. Then I did not jump into using it. I worked on my skills before trying it out on a bottom.

Bottoms are you aware too? Being too trusting can be dangerous. You should educate yourself. Know what you are getting into. It is ok to ask questions. And if a Top (Again same for Master or Dominant) get offended at your questions walk away, maybe even run. Talk deal it is ok. Set your limits.

C? Consent, it is the foundation and cornerstone of all we do. If you believe you have no consent seek help. I've written a lot on this subject. I can say a lot on the subject and there is a lot out there on consent. Oh, and important point that consent can be removed at any time.

K? Kink it is what we are about. What can I say we are kinky. Not normal so get over it.

Essay 11 Self-esteem

Self-esteem Do you like what you see in the mirror?

Is it a face you can trust?

Self-esteem is important to both Dominant and submissive. Shakespeare wrote, "To thine own self be true." This is a simple statement that will spark a host of reactions. Some people know themselves very well while others may not trust their own judgment. Yet some others will invest themselves solely on the opinion of what those around them are saying.

Building your self-esteem is important. You do it in baby steps.

Step 1 Acceptance:

The first step in acceptance, you accept the fact you don't like who, what or where you are in life. Own up to your mistakes and take pleasure in the things you have accomplished. In this acceptance of one's self, you are empowering yourself for the task ahead.

Someone once wrote acceptance was the key to all his problems. Once he had accepted his Alcoholism he could accept the changes that were needed.

In building or rebuilding self-esteem we must embrace who we are and realize that the Gods or God did not make junk. Simply put we must realize we belong. And only the arrogant will tell us we don't belong. We must learn how to tune out the negative voices and tune in the positive ones. And the way to determine what's negative and what is positive is this. Ask yourself this question, "Is what they are saying good for me or good for them?"

Step 2 Construction:

Once we have taken the 1st step we begin construction of the person. This is finding the wisdom to accept the things you cannot change but more importantly changing the things we can.

It is a myth that we can change those around us. And in D/s that myth is compounded by power exchange. For example, the Master may order his slave to quit smoking. (I have never smoked). What I understand that smoking is a very powerful addiction. And from listening to both smokers who have quit and can't quit, they all have one thing in common - the desire to quit. So, no matter how "Powerful" the Master says he/she is the slave can't quit unless the slave has the desire to quit.

Now we realize we can't change others any more than we can change the weather. But like the weather, if we don't like it we can change where we are. My point is this if the friends you have are having a bad influence on your construction than you change the friends. I have found from my own personal experience when you decide to embark on this path of self-discovery there are a lot of people who will "Tell YOU" how you should be. Listen to them but not everyone knows what is right for you. This is your journey, you have the power to decide on the changes you wish to make.

Step 3 Setting goals:

A good way to destroy your self-esteem is to set goals you cannot possibly obtain. Set small goals small steps. A good example of this is the dieter. Changing one's diet in one step can cause problems. Most successful dieters take small steps.

The same applies to setting goals to build your self-esteem. My hair is gray and I have a host of friends that like the gray. However, I don't like the gray. I feel better about myself if I am not gray. So, I dye the hair. A friend may not like the dyed hair but if truly a friend then it won't matter.

As you achieve each small goal, set larger ones. And a byproduct of this achievement will be you will find more and more confidence in yourself. And when you don't achieve your small goal, sit down and assess why. But don't assign blame, not to yourself or others. Just simply look for the reason. Some things just happen and it is not in our power to change it. One of the things that will damage your growth in self-acceptance and self-esteem is blaming yourself for your failure. This is not an excuse for averting the acceptance of responsibility. We should always be responsible for our actions. However, we do not need to punish ourselves for our mistakes. We should learn from those mistakes.

Step 4 Doing what you like:

Realize there is nothing wrong with doing what you like just to cause no harm to others. For example, I enjoy my steaks on the rare side. If I order the steak and it is presented on the good side I have a choice. I can accept what was given or I can send it back and get what I ordered.

I do not have the arrogance to say everything in life happens for a reason, nor do I believe that everything is random. However, I do believe what is important is the choice we make when it happens. Remember, the choices we make will dictate the life we lead. So, we need to learn to make good choices and be happy in what we do.

Step 5 The Path:

We must find our own path. This sounds simple but many on the path will tell you it is not. The path of self-discovery or paths to Enlightenment can be elusive. When we seek it, sometimes we will not find it. Or we don't seek and the path will appear.

That is why it is important to know yourself. Know what you find acceptable and what you will not accept. Often the answers we seek are within our own hearts. Remember Oz did not give the "tin man" anything he did not already have.

Some tips on finding your path. Meditate, don't pray just be. Next educate yourself, if you say, "I am Submissive" know what that means to you, not what it means to others but to yourself. Find the support of others of like mind. Last is an old hippie expression, "grow where you are planted

I hope this will help enlighten some of you and help you on your journey

Essay 12 The psychopath Dominant

To me, there are 3 types of abusers calling themselves Dominant.

1.) The armchair dominant

2.) The predator Dominant

3.) And the psychopath Dominant

Please note that even though I am writing this from the male point of view this is meant to be non-gender specific these traits can be in both Female & Male. Also, there is a very fine line between total M/s and abuse. I personally think the line is crossed when the submissive is no longer participating willingly or thriving in his or her submission. It is my firm believe as dominants we are responsible for the health and well-being of the submissive/slaves entrusted to us.

The first is the armchair "Dominant"

He will sit in his lounge chair and barks his orders. "Bitch where is my beer." Having no respect for the submissive "Bitch quiet your brats" more like the Archie Bunker (now I know that there are submissive/slaves who thrive on this.) and there lies the difference. Is the submissive thriving or slowly dying inside. Is the submissive smile as they were the bear a result of the pleasure of serving or have they spit in the beer before serving it?

To me, the armchair dominant wants to enjoy the benefits of the D/s relationship and doesn't want to do any of the work. This is also the lazy dominant. (I'm sorry I believe to keep good submissives this requires WORK on the Dominants part) This is one of the differences between abuse and M/s. A smart submissive will one day bring the collar with the beer and move on. However, this won't matter to the armchair Dominant he will just move into the next willing victim.

The next one the predator Dominant;

This is the person who for some sick twisted reason looks for prey to destroy. We all know the "MO" of the predator. Matter of fact I could type a name right now and both Lady Devon & Sir Edwin would know who I was talking about. His (yes male) MO is always the same; he has a fake photo of himself at the place he will give you as a place of employment. He has an excuse why he doesn't attend munches. But he has been in the lifestyle 100 years yet he can't name any one of the leaders in the local community. However, he will always have an excuse why you can't get in touch with a past submissive. His main prey is the "new be" or "an innocent". I believe we all know the type and his methods.

Last and I believe the most dangerous of all the abusers are the psychopath Dominant.

Why do I think this person is so dangerous? Because they are unaware of what they doing. I believe both the Lazy & Predator are aware of what they are doing. But the "Psychopath" I firmly believe they are oblivious to the damage they are causing. And that is what makes them so dangerous. It is never their fault. There is no accountability for their actions. Decisions are made in haste with no forethought. Then when something goes wrong it was the submissive's fault. They are good at hiding their miss deeds

Now how do you protect the submissive from this type of Dominant? The answer is to educate the submissive. They should be aware (the submissive) of what they are looking for. When Sir Jim's d first approached me for training I had a choice. It was obvious to me she had no clue I took it upon myself she called her safe call. I made sure she knew we were meeting in a very public place. At the time and she did not know it but I arranged the meet in a restaurant where I was well known. It was the same place we held the Zephyrhills munch. When we met I could see the word victim written on her forehead. No, she was ripe for the picking. But she got lucky. After completion of training and I took the role of protector I allowed her to look for a Dominant of her own. I knew she was well trained in the signs. One of my rules as protector was the dominant had to write and ask permission to meet her or even call her on the phone. (I wish I kept some of the responses they were downright funny)

I feel bad when a submissive comes to me feeling used and abused because they did not know what to look for. But I feel it is the responsibility of the dominant to educate the submissive. If you are a total Master/slave relationship it is OUR duty to see that the slave understands their requirements.

Essay 14 The Bully Dominant.

Years ago, I wrote the Psychopath Dominant. It has been published on the internet and read by many people. I've described 3 types of Dominants. Those are the armchair dominant, The predator Dominant, And the psychopath Dominant. Today I'd like to introduce to you the latest abuser to the BDSM lifestyle. He or she I call the "Bully Dominant".

Here we go, you say to the bully dominant I am submissive and the bully says no you are my slave. You say I have my limits and the bully says, you are my slave and I don't allow you to have limits. You say I am not bisexual and the bully says you will have sex with another one of your same sex. You say I am not poly and the bully tells you that you are one of his many slaves. The bully will force himself on you. He/she will not consider your feelings. The bully will not respect your limits. Why do you give into the bully dominant? First, you are desperate for a Master so you put your needs aside to meets his/her needs. You find yourself doing things you know you would never do because you have been forced to leave your principals behind.

The bully has convinced you that is the way of BDSM. You are not sure so you allow yourself to be bullied into crossing your own hard limits. You will not be happy but the bully has convinced you it is all about him/her and their needs.

Another reason you go with the bully is that he/she is good in bed. A relationship built on just sex is not a good relationship. I know my first marriage was built on sex. We were good in bed. But it did not last, we got bored. There is more to life than sex. BDSM isn't always about sex. Yes, it is a sexual lifestyle but there is also the power exchange. There is no power exchange with the bully dominant.

The third reason is love. you don't understand what love is. Or you confuse love and sex or you are just so lonely even a bully is acceptable. But you are not happy, you fight but you will not allow yourself to walk away because you think you are in love. But the bully doesn't really love you. The bully only loves him/herself and what he/she can get.

Abuse is not loved. Love is kind. Love is understanding. Love respects you. Love will care if you are happy. Love doesn't force him/her self on you. If you say you are a submissive love will listen and respect you as submissive. If you say you are not bisexual love will not force you into same-sex activity.

Warning this is on this type of abuser. Runaway doesn't walk away. You have been warned. Take your time get to know the dominant you have interest in. whether you are a slave, sub or bottom don't rush. Always be up front. Know what you want. Realize you as the submissive/slave you have all the power. And be aware of the types of the abuser is. And how this is not BDSM!!

Essay 15 Honor

What does it mean to you? How much honor should you have? How does one define such a broad concept?

When I sat down to write this I realized what honor means to me may not have the same meaning to you. For example, a person asks for help my personal honor says to try and help. That may not apply to someone else. They may think is this going to bite me in the ass? Or they may think what benefit do I get out of it?

Honor is such a shade of gray. Some things are black and white, for example, never kick someone when they are down. Or you don't cause harm.

Having a code of honor is important to a Dominant. So, what is your code of honor?

My code is never causing harm. Be honest. Be helpful. Do to others what you would have them do to you. Never use and abuse, live life to the fullest with harming other, in the words of Rodney Dangerfield in "Back to School", "Look out for number 1 without stepping in number 2"

Essay 16 Masters and slaves

Many M/s relationships rely on the M/s contract. First "Contracts" are not legal documents. If used in court they are used to convict you of domestic abuse. So, what good is a contract? A contract can be used as a relationship guide. It can guide you on what you will do and what you will not do. It can be to define limits both hard and soft. I've written them. A contract is also used to spell out duties and responsibilities of both parties. There are sample contracts all over the internet. I have samples on my computer. I've used them and I haven't used them. My last M/s relationship was without a contract and that was a mistake. From now on if I enter into an M/s relationship there will be a contract. The contract can be the source of great debate. That is not what I'm trying to cause here. A contact may not benefit you or your relationship. That is OK. A lot of relationships don't use them. I just think they make communication better. We will talk about communication soon.

Now a word to slaves and subs. You have a right to set limits. If you think you have no right to limits you are mistaken. If the Master/Dominant tells you, you have no right to limits find another master or dominant. Limits should be negotiated up front before the contract for slave. And for subs during the whole relationship. Everyone has limits. When I hear a slave say she has no limits I think she/he is either uneducated, desperate or mentally ill. I'm not going to debate this issue either. I have 34years' experience that says different. Slaves/subs educate yourselves Do your homework on a potential Master. Don't be afraid to ask for a reference or 3. Ask where they learned their skills. Don't accept "life experience". Ask about other relationships and why it did not work. Don't talk to the Ex, he/she might be bitter and hateful. When my 3rd wife and broke up in 2001 she was very bitter and went on a mission to drive me from the BDSM community. In 2008, I ran into her and she was still bitter and angry. What did I do to make her so angry? I took $500 from the joint account. She wanted me to leave with nothing. The $500 wasn't half which I had a right to. she would show up at munches to scare off friends. But it did not work because people knew the truth. I did lose some friends but I don't need friends like that. Don't be in a rush, I've been in a rush and it did not last. But for some it did last. I'm saying it is a gamble when you meet yesterday and are collared today. Take time to get to know him/her. See what else you have in common. Most Masters don't live in leather. Real life can get in the way. Don't put your master above your children. The proper order is God, Family career if you have one and then Master. Kids come first. Now I'm not saying don't involve him with your kids. My last relationship had 3 teenage kids. I tried to take the role of step-dad. And I gave advice on my parenting style because I raised a son. But the advice was asked for not forced. I also involved the women in my life to help with my son. Back in 2002 I had a crisis and a woman who was like a sister and she was a slave stepped to take Jr under a wing and became a mother to him. to this day she calls him her son. And she was a better mother to him than his own mother. But Jr always came first. A master may not be comfortable in the role as step-parent and that is on. Never is Master the master of your children never.

Back to M/s, Masters you're responsible for your slave's needs. Don't sit in the chair and just give orders. Be active. I've made the mistake and it did not work. Your slave has needs, including to be happy. Her/his service should make them happy but it doesn't always do. I wrote the ten responsibilities of the Dominant. But I did not add happiness there. After a lot of thought, I have come to the conclusion that it is our job to make them happy. Teach yourself these skills. Attend classes, demos, and clubs. I am a bondage master but never suspended someone. Once I suspended the first wife about a foot off the bed and we fucked but that was the only time and she was a small woman. It was at a club called Master's Quest where I learned the basics to suspension. Now I am confident in suspending a bigger woman.

Masters, it is no shame to admit you don't know something. Don't pretend you know everything. You are human and your slave should except your shortcomings. I do not pretend I have all the answers. If did I'd be better at maintaining a relationship. I am in therapy to learn how to have a better relationship. Most people say a relationship is 50/50, but I think a relationship should be 100% both ways. I have 33 years' experience, and I am still learning. We should as Masters keep learning. Sub/slave beware of the person that says he has all the answers, or you have no right to question. That is a major red flag. Subs/slaves you have a right to know and ask questions. I productive relationship is based on growth. Growth together as master and slave. Masters don't be afraid of growth. Growth and self-improvement are healthy. And masters your slave/sub has a right to a healthy relationship. Masters, you have a right to be pleased with your sub/slave. But don't set the bar so high they always fail to please.

Encourage growth and learning, a smart slave/sub is a good slave or sub. Teach your slave/sub, don't assume anything even with a well-trained slave/sub. They may have been trained differently. You might require a sex slave and she/he is trained to be a domestic. Interview each other. Before jumping into the collar get to know him/her. Use the collar system, the collar of concertation, training collar, and formal collar. Masters, I don't care if she is a supermodel be careful. She could be the best fuck you ever had don't base your relationship in sex. I did that with my first marriage. My first wife and I were good in bed. But that is where it ended. I wanted a kid and she did not want any kids. See where I am going? I may not be an expert on maintaining a relationship but I am good at failing them. No, I don't say that with pride. It is my weakness and I am learning to be better at it.

Communication is a very important element in any relationship. When communication breaks down the end of the relationship might not be far behind. Masters, slaves/sub need to communicate. Masters if you think all you should do is bark orders you are sadly mistaken. That is not an M/s relationship. Keep a journal. I keep a journal. Masters, you should read your slave's journal. But you should not punish for what he/she might say. Let her/him write without fear. Masters keep your own journal and you don't have to let the slave read it. I keep a private journal I've been keeping one for years. Put away are journals that date back to the 90s. Masters always make your communications clear. Don't give vague orders. Like I want my coffee at 9 am. Let him/her know how you take it and how you want it presented. I'm not saying micro-manage your slave/sub. However, some slaves/subs crave micro-management. More power to you. Let them make mistakes. Teach them how to improve rather than punish. Personally, if I have to punish I feel like I've failed to communicate. Punishment should be a low priority. Unless you have the punishment game dynamic.

The relationship whether it is vanilla, D/s or M/s is complex. Don't try and make it simple, that might backfire on you. Learn and grow together. Notice I did not address top and bottom because that is different. To me, top and bottom are more about the play. I 'm not educated on the dynamic. I've played with different subs and slaves but that was either temporary or with a sub/slave I was in a relationship with.

So, we covered negotiation, contract, communication, and needs. BDSM activities are not needed in the M/s relationship. But they can add to the fun. Be mindful of safety first. If you do rope bondage have something handy to cut the ropes in case of something going wrong. Ex-wife #3 and I loved bondage and she loved dressing up. So, we were playing in the kitchen on this bar. I was trying a partial suspension when she slipped and fell. Nylons are slippery. I had to cut the rope. Things happen, best be ready. If you are using cuffs leather or steel use the right cuff. If doing a flogging be aware of the "No Hit Zones". Same applies to a whip. Floggers and whips can cause damage. You can break bone with them or damage kidneys. If you are doing hot wax be sure you are using the right type of wax. Some candles contain oil and they can burn the skin. Your goal is to cause pain or some level of pain or erotica. Do not cause harm. If you are doing mind play be sure to know the proper triggers. It is important to have play times. My 3rd ex-wife/sub had playtimes, we made it a point to play twice a week. Once I had her tied and we were playing and the school called. I could use the line she's tied up right now can I take a message.

I know this isn't very scriptural or spiritual today but we are also a BDSM group. And so is Master/slave Dominant/submissive relationships. I know I wrote this to Masters and Slaves but it also can apply to the Dominant/sub relationship too. I've had this writer's block when it came to BDSM. I've put my manuscript away for the time being and just wrote spiritual things and I've enjoyed writing the spiritual writings. But BDSM, M/s or D/s are also important parts of our lives. We need to learn to balance the spiritual and the relationship. Keep your relationship with God and your relationships with others. Masters have friends, maybe have a mentor. I believe in mentorship. I have a friend who is a Christian Master who I turn to for advice. We've known each other for over a decade or more. Subs/slave if a master has no friends be careful I would suggest finding someone else. I don't give a damn how hot he/she is. Isolation is what an abuser does. Subs/slave have friends and a mentor who isn't a master. I don't think a dominant should mentor a sub or a sub mentor a dominant. Yes, there are those who do this and are successful at it. I just don't do it.

Final thought, first this is all my opinion based on my 34 years of experience take it or leave it. You may disagree with some of it or most of it. Masters, you might hate my style of M/s and that is ok That is OK if I can reach one-person Master or slave it is worth it. A lot of injury and mistakes come from a lack of education. Now I'm not suggesting you become a submissive before taking on a submissive. That debate well brings a lot of anger. I'm saying Masters/Dominants train yourselves, take classes go to demos. Slave/submissive I'm saying educate yourself please do go with someone because he looks good. Be smart know yourself, know your limits and be picky. Many mistakes are made out of desperation. One of my fantasies is to suspend a masochist and cover her with whip marks. I have not attempted that because I don't have a masochist or a place to do it safely. My advice is based on 34 years of experience. I've made many a mistake. I've learned from those. I've been robbed twice. One time after being in this for years. I trusted and I was robbed of 90$. Things happen we all fuck up. But learn from those fuck ups. Listen, read, learn I suggest the book "SM101" to every new person. But I believe everyone should read it. I have a copy and refer to it all the time.

It seems I forgot safe words. whether you are submissive or slave you should have a safe word. If someone tells you different run away don't walk away.

Essay 17 Punishment vs. discipline

You need DISCIPLINE!

SA.M.? Spunky?

Let's play the punishment game.

You need to be punished.

Is there a difference between the two? What is that difference?

There is a difference between punishment & discipline. I find the confusion between punishment & discipline common with most new people in the BDSM D/s scene today. I try to teach both new Dominants and submissive/slaves this difference.

You need DISCIPLINE!

I have discipline in my life. Most of us do. A good dominant should have discipline in their life. After all, if you can't master yourself how can you master someone else? Paul the Christian leader knew this and put it to use in choosing church leaders. He mandated in one of his letters that a church pastor or deacon should be married with children. His principle was if you can't manage your own home how could you lead a church? This same principle applies to D/s. How can you master a slave if you can't master yourself? This doesn't mean you should be in total control of yourself 100% of the time? No, it doesn't it means to have basic self-control. However, it does take Discipline to keep control. This takes training on our part.

A good example of self-discipline would be getting up every morning at the same time each and every day. It could mean running every morning or eating right. What makes some pay his/her bills while the other will spend the grocery money on a new pair of boots? Discipline could be jogging each morning or having a daily meditation.

So, what are the Disciplines in your life? Why are they there? How did you install them?

Giving a submissive a bedtime would be a form of discipline. A good discipline for your trainee would be the keeping of a Journal. A timely-kept journal is a good way to get the submissive in the habit of expressing her/himself on paper rather than acting out. It is a good communication tool for you the trainer. Every trainee I keep I require them to keep a journal. There is no negation this is a requirement. Something your submissive needs to learn is submission is not always fun. Your job is to push their limits, make them grow. And if they refuse to grow then maybe it is time to move on.

S.A.M:

What is a SAM (Smart Ass Masochist)? What is the difference between a SAM and spunky?

You and your submissive are at the local play party and she does something to embarrass you and this calls for a caning. While you are laying her out she seems to enjoy the punishment. Meet SAM not really a submissive more of a bottom masochist. Some people are in this for the pleasure of pain. And there is nothing wrong with that. What becomes wrong is the embarrassment the dominant will have among his/her peers.

Playing the "punishment game":

The what? What is the punishment game? This is the game where the Dominant will set up the submissive to fail in order to be punished. This game can be very damaging to the submissive mentally.

Submissives/slave thrive on pleasing Master. If they are always displeasing Master then it causes their self-respect to break down. The desire of the submissive is to please. This is at the core of their being. a good Dominant knows this and works to build this sense of worth.

If you are dominant with a sadistic side then let the submissive know. Even if the submissive/slave is not in pain, the submissive/slave will derive pleasure from the act of pleasing. And this will build self-worth. Your submissive is valued and should be treated as such.

You need to be punished:

Why punish? What not use positive reinforcement?

Punishing should be a last resort. But sometimes in the D/s relationship, it is necessary. It should be a last resort not the first.

But why punish?

A submissive/slave will punish their selves fore worse the thing you, as the dominant will ever can. But this self-flogging is worse than anything you can come up with. The problem is this is very self-damaging. Punishment offers closure. It put an end to the problem that caused the punishment to begin with. Remember to take no pleasure in punishing. But like a lot of things, it takes self-discipline.

One submissive I was training did something wrong when she broke discipline. So, I as her dominant & trainer had to punish her. Well, this person is a "Pain Slut" so I did not choose pain like a flogging to punish her.

"Now you lost me here...lol. If I refused to get on that cross to be whipped or refused to go to bed when told.... wouldn't I need discipline? Not that I would ever do that."

So, to clear this misunderstanding up the "bedtime" would be the discipline. The refusal would call for punishment.

Punishment is a part of D/s:

This is the true marker between a submissive, slave and bottom. A submissive will allow punishment but will they to control where a slave will accept it. However, a bottom may not. The bottom will even ask for release over being punished. Punishing should never be looking for. I personally feel if you can find a different corrective measure. This is where Discipline comes in. for example the "Bedtime". You may want to change the time to re-enforce this as to taking away computer time.

Ways to punish:

It is not a good idea to punish a pain slut with a hard beating. You may wish to punish by withholding the beating. I personally will remove something the submissive may enjoy. For example, the submissive may enjoy recreational masturbation well this would become a quickly restricted activity. I don't like the removal of the presence of the Dominant. I think when you ignore them you are closing the lines of communication. You should always be there for the slave/submissive. And to ignore them would cause harm to the mental health of the submissive. Plus, it may stat SAM behavior. The submissive/slave will do anything to get your Attention.

Rules to punish by:

The punishment should always fit the crime. Always. First, sit down and explain why this punishment is being administered. Don't talk about just explaining why. Example: Slave your bedtime is 9 pm and you were on the computer until 10 pm for the third time. Don't allow an excuse. If you feel you want to know the reason why. That is the Dominant's choice. But don't allow excuses for unacceptable behavior. Even if you punish with pain explain why. Personally, I will not punish with something I enjoy. For example, if I enjoy flogging I will not punish with a flogging.

Last when the punishing time is up. That is the end of it. Never bring it up unless it is a constant infraction. Like the bedtime example, if you punish & use a re-enforced discipline and you still have the behavior then you have a bigger problem.

A final thought.

One thing to consider when you are the Trainer or Master/Mistress some bad behaviors may be out of your control.

Behavior like drinking or smoking I know some of us like to think we can correct anything but remember you are still mortal and your submissive/slave is still human.

Essay 18 Elements of a relationship

Whether it be Master/slave, Dominant/submissive or vanilla these elements are essential.

First honesty, second trust, third communication, fourth support, fifth respect and last affection.

There really isn't an order of importance. They are equal, and when one brakes down they all seem to break down.

Honesty, being honest with your feelings, wants, desires, needs and hope just to name a few. Both of you need to be honest. Self-honesty is important, don't lie to yourself. Many often lie to themselves about their feeling or what they want or what their true needs are.

Trust, this is something earned. Yes, trust should be earned. Don't give your trust away no matter how sexy they are. Many times, I've jumped into a relationship and given away trust. I suggest you don't just jump into a blind relationship no matter how sexy they are.

There are two kinds of trust - basic trust and unconditional trust. Basic trust is something we give freely and almost daily. We trust the store clerk or bank teller with our transaction. We trust our teachers with the education of our kids. This is basic but not unconditional, there are conditions attached to that trust. For example, the trusted teacher has the education to teach; the bank teller is bonded. However, unconditional trust is something that should be earned, and when broken it is hard to win back. You give it in small increments. A good way to earn trust is by demonstrating your ability to be trustworthy.

So how do you earn unconditional trust? You keep your word. You respect hard limits. And you communicate, communicate and communicate. This trust goes deeper, the kind that means you would trust your very life (for REAL) to someone, is not a trust that can be built in just days or weeks. This much deeper level of trust can often take years to establish.

Communication, not only do you need to communicate it needs to be honest, open and often. There are different methods of communication. You can keep a journal. For those in M/s or D/s relationships try the "the slave journal". The submissive/slave writes open honest feeling without the worry or repercussion. Have time out. That is when you step out of the rolls of Master/slave or Dominant/submissive and talk on a human level.

Respect, this too is earned. So, let's talk about respect. A good Dominant/Master should have respect for his/her submissive/slave. Also, he/she should have self-respect. Having the respect of your slave/submissive is easy - you just earn it. You earn respect by keeping your word, not causing harm, and showing respect to your submissive/slave.

The dictionary defines self-respect as proper esteem or regard for the dignity of one's character. Proper esteem meaning good self-esteem and not "Dom-Ego." You build character by doing the right things, like causing no harm and having a good moral center. I think self-respect is necessary. Necessary for a good relationship and necessary to be a good Dominant/Master. The way we respect ourself has a direct bearing on how we respect others. You may say you only respect those who earn it.

Affection yes being affectionate. Little gifts such as flowers or a new toy. Show an interest in what he/she is into. A kiss, a hug, letting them know how you feel. This is a hard one for me. Because I've never given it much thought. But affection is important to the relationship. It lets them know their importance.

Support I left out support. It is important that you support each other's interests. Have things in common. Have things that are different. But support each other.

The friendship I would add being friends with him/her. Start out as friends. Too many want the quick fix. Jump right into the relationship as lovers or something else.

Essay 19 Perceptions and misconceptions

The observance of people can be a fascinating topic. Yesterday I needed to go to the bank and make a quick deposit. It would have been a simple matter the drive-thru and home. However, I decided to make it an experience and not for just for me but for those who I would come into contact with.

So, I showered but I left the morning stubble for a hard-core look. Then I put on my black jeans, blue shirt and my black leather vest. My boots completed the look, if a person did not know better he/she would have thought I was headed to the local biker bar or BDSM club.

I did not drive but took the local city bus to downtown. It was lunchtime and all the lawyers and secretaries were on their lunch break. I did my "Saturday Night Fever" strut as I walked to the bank. 4 lawyers were walking behind me rather fast I could hear their conversation in the past. I wondered what they were thinking as they very politely past. Maybe one was thinking, is he my next client? Maybe one thought, there is my next defendant? They said, "excuse me" as they passed my 6 foot 2-inch 270-pound black leather clad ass. I noticed a few ladies giving double takes I do clean up nicely. (Or so I have been told.) I walked into the bank and was quickly greeted by 2 or 3 people. After all, how many Bad Asses come in at lunchtime. I did notice the security guard watching me and I did notice another guard come on the floor as I walked up to the teller. I removed my sunglasses and smiled at the young woman. I dropped off the money and left I looked the security guard in the eyes and smiled. I wonder if he was deciding where to shoot first.

Well, it was lunchtime and I was in the mood for a good slice of pizza. So, with my "Saturday Night Fever" strut I made my way to a nice little pizza place. The waiter was standing outside he tried not to make eye contact but he failed. I sat outside and ordered. I watched the people watch me. I was amazed that one woman sat across the street from my table and watched me. I'd look at her and she would quickly look away. Maybe she was one of us but did not want to say anything.

After I finished my lunch, I tipped the waiter and moved on. As I walked back to the bus stop I spotted a homeless man sitting on the street with his cup out. As I walked past, he moved his cup close to himself and took a submissive posture. I walked about 3 steps past, turned, and walked back. I gave him a buck and walked on. He was shocked.

We all have Perceptions and misconceptions of how things should look sound and feel. A big man in black with a leather vest and biker boots must be a "Bad Ass" Downtown this Bad Ass must be a felon. To some maybe, I was a fantasy of a freer life. Maybe to the guard at thee back, I was a very real danger. To the woman watching me eat maybe I was someone that she had seen online. After all, I do have my ad on http://bondage.com

In addition, the same applies to the BDSM lifestyle we have Perceptions and misconceptions, a slave should sound soft, and a Dom should be Domly. What the hell is "Domly" anyway? We perceive from a predetermined way of thinking. Some think in a box $x + y = Z$ when we should try to think outside of the box. Big guy, black leather, and jeans = badass.

So maybe next time I put on my ugly Hawaiian shirt, (my Jimmy Buffett look) my leather sandals and look like a tourist and attend the local munch.

Essay 20 Questions you should ask anyone:

How much experience do you have?

Are you married? Or in a relationship?

What is your health like?

How do you support yourself?

Where do you live, house or apartment?

Are you active in the local community?

Why are you not active in the local community?

Our first meeting in a public place?

I don't play or have sex on the first date, do you?

These are questions I suggest you ask.

These are the questions I will ask you.

OH, don't be in a rush, I'm not. When you rush you make mistakes.

Essay 21 Red Flags

The following are red flags or warning signs. They do always mean one is an abuser or predator but these are the lines they use and should be a warning look out this person is not always honest.

Yes, I'm married and my wife/husband is not into this.

Oh, I have no use for the community I'm more of a private person.

Oh yes, I have had this nickname or that nickname I like to keep changing them.

Oh, you want to meet in a public place? Sure, but can we stop at my motel room first I forgot something.

Oh, you want to call my wife/husband? Sure, but they are not available.

Oh, I don't go to munches I just don't want to get caught and lose my Job

For the Female Dominants. Oh, Mistress, my wife does not understand my need to do service.

Please don't ask others about me, no one understands my style of D/s.

Of course, I will train you and you will be completely trained in one night.

I am just not a joiner.

I am the master and as the slave, you have no right to question. That is a common red flag.

Essay 22 Suggestions to the new submissive/slave

So, you have discovered your sub/slave side. These suggestions are for both.

First, remember this is a power exchange. You have all the power not the Dominant. This is a lifestyle of consent. Always keep in mind you have the power to say no. Even the slave has the power to walk away. If a Master tells you, you have no rights. He is wrong you have to power to end the relationship and walk away. And if he/she will not let you end the relationship he/she is not a master but an abuser. I would suggest involving the police and courts. They never side with the so-called master. I remember reading once where a master brought a contract into court. The court threw the book at him.

Consent is the cornerstone of all we do.

Before you go running out to find a Dominant of your own I suggest you educate yourself. Learn the difference between this and abuse. I suggest lots of reading. Start out with SM 101 and The Loving Dominant. You may desire a trainer. This Is a good idea if you find a real trainer. A lot of abusers use training as a ruse to get sex or play. Be careful who you select as a trainer.

What is Training

Training is not a sexual act. It is not learning how to perform simple oral sex. However, there is a sexual component to training. Training is not teaching someone how to be submissive. Real life slavery is immoral and illegal. You cannot make someone be something they are not. And it will be said repeatedly you cannot train someone to be submissive or slave. But you can train a submissive/slave to be superior.

Training, this is something needed for every good dominant & submissive. Proper training can cement the bond between Master and slave, Mistress and her boy, the Dominant and the submissive. One of the most important things you will ever do is train a submissive. You will be molding this person in the D/s BDSM lifestyle. You will be laying the foundation for this person. You are providing them with the tools they will need to survive in this BDSM world. This person has trusted you with their education. This is there training they will need to serve their future master. You are responsible for their protection. And you are responsible for their behavior both in public and in private. Do not take training lightly.

Also, there are those who will accuse you of using the person you are training. If you're a Dominant of honor there is no need to respond to such accusations. Remember the proof of the pudding is in the eating. Simply put, your works will silence their words.

Last, not all you train will complete your training nor will they live up to your expectations. Just be honest, respectful and do the best you are able to do. And remember above all let honor be your guide.

Should every sub/slave be trained? The short answer is you. But this is something you may want your Dominant to do.

Next, I suggest a mentor. A mentor is not a sex partner. There is nothing wrong with sex partners or play partners. One of my best friends is also a play partner. A mentor is some who you can seek advice from. A mentor should not be a future dominant. I suggest a sub have a sub mentor, and a slave has a slave mentor. Next you both submissive & slave have the right to negotiate. Yes, slave girls before entering into a slave contract you have the right to negotiate. If the master says no you don't run away don't walk away but run. This is all about consent. Every true Dominant respect consent.

Next, get involved in the local community. Abusers tend to isolate you from others. No matter how private you are you should have some community involvement. Attend a munch. A much is a safe place to meet others. Also, make friends.

Last be careful. Be picky, have self-respect, and one last thought something that happened to me. I was in a rush to practice bondage when I first go into this 28 years ago. To make a long story short I found myself tied up and robbed. Don't BE IN A RUSH. Always put your family first.

New submissive/slave best of luck and always seek out people like me with knowledge and experience.

Essay 23 The beauty of bondage

I love music, artists like Mozart or John Lennon, swing time to hard rock and even the music we flog to. However, I cannot write or play (except play the Radio) music. Bondage is a symphony of ropes or chains enhancing the human form. Whether the bondage is Shibari (Japanese rope bondage), Shinju (breast bondage), Karada (the body harness) or a good old fashion hog tie, it requires mastery and skill much like the concert piano. For me, the skill came as natural as cooking or writing poetry (2 more arts).

There are those of us who see beauty in the whip marks we leave on the bottom of our slaves. For others in our way, beauty is the presentation of a Gorian Serve. For me, it is the beauty of the layer of ropes. The time it takes to do the bindings. Much like cooking bondage takes time and preparation. You must know the body type you are working with. You just do not place ropes anywhere. You need to allow the human form to inspire you.

A few years ago, I became fascinated with Shibari style suspending. This was a skill I had to master. I did not join an Internet group to learn nor did I rent a movie or buy a book. I went to the local Shibari Master and I learned. I asked questions like why did you use nylon and not cotton ropes.

Oh, know some who find bondage boring and it is ok. I think one of the greatest things is to suspend someone, play with them and top it off with good old fashion sex.

Learning bondage requires patience. I know in the "microwave-cooking world" that is not a word some like. Patience like skill is something we learn. Bondage is turn on it is the B in BDSM.

Essay 24 Manners Common Courtesy BDSM

It started with a simple apology for unacceptable language from a submissive in training. The posts continued and off the topic. So, I started thinking. Hum is it dangerous for a Dominant to start thinking?

A few years ago, my X and I were at a local munch. The host of the munch was a submissive in a well-known house. I was impressed at the manners and movements of this Dominant and his submissives. Yes, he had two and both were well behaved and in a protocol. For those who know what "second protocol" is that is what they were in. To say these to submissives were impressive was an understatement. Then the unthinkable happened. On to the women poured a pitcher of ice tea in my lap. Anyway the submissive of 15+ years in the lifestyle was horrified. However good manners prevailed.

I made it a point to get to know these 3 people. Later this Dominant would become my best friend and the submissive who baptized me in ice tea is now a sister and about 3 years ago I became a member of House Ursa.

I understand a person's right to use "Bad Language". However how many people would want the waitress to ask, "May I take your order"? Or would you rather someone say, "oh what the F*&%$ do you want"? Would you really eat a place like that? Think about it I have heard that even professionals use this type of gutter talk. Well maybe I'm sheltered but every job I ever had using that type of speech was grounds for discipline or dismissal. Even when I worked in nursing for those 9 years I never saw a doctor address a patient in a rude manner and most doctors who knew me knew I would not put up with that type of behavior. And yes, I have a doc or to cures me out at 2 am when I needed to call them but most of them only did it once. I guess being 6'2'' and looking like a crazed biker most of the time had something to do with it.

But I will confess I am not an actor or porn star and those are the only 2 occupations I can think of where foul language is acceptable. Oh, I forgot rock star to seems a lot of today's rock use the F-word in every other line.

First, our standard is not the vanilla. And yes, I know I can be a real D/s snob. But that is real life. In a real-life party or event rude behavior, improper touching, or inappropriate language will get you ejected from the event. Maybe it is just the crowd I hang out with.

I feel manners and common courtesy are going the way of the dinosaurs. Or is it just an Internet thing. I don't understand why some feel they must be rude or behave inappropriately.

Essay 25 BDSM Play:

Induction

There are those who believe BDSM is not necessary to training but I feel it is. I believe that the submissive should have a basic foundation of BDSM play for safety reasons and a way to make personal choices.

Next to the Dominant reading this. I suggest before you pick up a flogger or a riding crop you make sure you have mastered that skill. The toys we play with can cause broken bones can cause permanent injury even death. READING a book on How To is not mastering a skill. Watching Someone Else do it is not Mastering A Skill! Having someone teach & train you is mastering a skill. Know your limits.

BDSM is not just a spectator sport.

Lesson 1. My toys.

The submissive/slave may or may not have seen some of the toys in your toy bag. Some toy bags are a little different than others. But most have the basics floggers, riding crops, and straps. After all, there is Pain (with a frown) and there is Pain (with a smile) which place do you want to take your trainee? I prefer Pain with the smile.

When introducing toys take it slowly. The goal is to have your trainee become friends with Mr. flogger or Ms. Riding Crop not to frighten the novice. Let her/him feel them, touch them hold them. And if a toy frightens the trainee then don't push the toy on her/him. Just smile and put it back in the bag. Remember some of the things we use to bring pleasure may have been in the past used to bring terror to the submissive.

Lesson 2. The feel of the toy

Don't strip your trainee and beat the hell out of her/him unless you want to lose the trainee. It pisses me off when I hear stories how a dominant will take a new person and just beat them with no control. Kind of makes me want to put them on a cross. (Rant Done)

What I like is to have a gentle touch, show the trainee on his/her arm or threw his/his clothing. I will even hit myself on the arm to show that this device of torture can bring great pleasure.

Lesson 3. The first session

Give the trainee some time before you jump right into the first session. You may even want to have a friend sit in or have one of the trainee's friends sit in. Be realistic the first session should be slow and easy for the submissive who has never felt the kiss of a flogger.

1.) Before the session tell the submissive your plans. Explain the toys you plan to use. Explain the stages of the session.

2.) Explain the use of code or safe words. I would never play with a trainee without a save word.

3.) Never assume the submissive understands. I remember the first time I felt the sting of the riding crop. I did not understand what the Lady was talking about. See starting out on the bottom does have benefit.

4.) Be gentle! Start with the trainee's clothing on if you need. Remember this first session is for her/him, not you.

5.) Control your own sexual desires.

6.) DO NOT USE BONDAGE! The submissive must feel relaxed. If the trainee desires bondage use brake-a-way cuffs or lose and easy ropes. Always put safety first.

7.) Last be aware that the trainee may not use a code word so watch him/her closely and if you have a doubt stop. Don't just blow it off.

After the session is over and you are done with the aftercare sit down talk about everything. She submissive may need to cry the submissive may need to laugh. Just be open because almost anything can happen.

Note: some want D/s without BSDM and that is ok. Some Like BDSM without the D/s that is ok. BUT my own opinion is why can't we enjoy both? But I am one of those sic puppy's that what it all.

Essay 26 Crossing limits a true story.

This was written in 2002

Crossing limits, a true story.

About a year ago a submissive crossed my path then she became my trainee. Step one for me with a new trainee is the education of toys. What each toy is for and the different effect a toy may or may not have on her body. Step II is making a limits list.

This is the story of a beautiful painful strap and how in 6 months' time it moved from the hard limit list to the "more please Sir" list.

This strap was off limits because it resembled an implement of childhood discipline. I listen and I removed the strap from the toy bag. But I displayed the strap where it could be seen. Over the next 3 months as my submissive in training started to turn into a "pain slut" she started eyeing the strap. Then she started asking about it. As she learned about the different toys she learned that in my toy bag there were toys being used that were far more painful. A month later she asked me to put the strap back in the toy bag.

Did I use the strap the same night? NO, the time was not right. When this time was right I used it. Today that strap is an important part of D's life. Because it represents growth change and what the possibilities are when you have an open mind.

How do you know when the time is right? You need to know you're submissive to answer that.

Essay 27 Trust

A good relationship is built upon a good foundation. A good foundation is made of solid stones. The cornerstone is consent. Other foundation stones are trust, respect, and commitment. Communication is the cement that binds the stones together.

Let's talk about trust. The dictionary says it well: Assured reliance on the character, strength, or truth of someone or something.

There are two kinds of trust - basic trust and unconditional trust. Basic trust is something we give freely and almost daily. We trust the store clerk or bank teller with our transaction. We trust our teachers with the education of our kids. This is basic but not unconditional, there are conditions attached to that trust. For example, the trusted teacher has the education to teach; the bank teller is bonded. However, unconditional trust is something that should be earned, and when broken it is hard to win back. You give it in small increments. A good way to earn trust is by demonstrating your ability to be trustworthy.

So how do you earn unconditional trust? You keep your word. You respect hard limits. And you communicate, communicate and communicate. This trust goes deeper, the kind that means you would trust your very life (for REAL) to someone, is not a trust that can be built in just days or weeks. This much deeper level of trust can often take years to establish.

In order for a submissive to be able to give of themselves to a Dominant, there should be unconditional trust in all aspects of the relationship.

Trust in D/s should work both ways. The sub/slave should earn your trust as well. She/he should communicate honestly with you about her/his needs, wants, and desires. As the Dominant, you should meet the needs of the slave/sub. But wants and desires are open to negotiation.

Essay 28 The ten responsibilities of the dominant

1.) To safeguard the welfare of his/her submissive/slave

2.) To meet the needs of his/her submissive/slave (Not the desires)

3.) To educate and train his/her submissive/slave

4.) To protect his/her submissive/slave

5.) To honor & respect his/her submissive/slave

6.) To ensure the safety of his/her submissive/slave

7.) To prepare his/her submissive/slave is something should happen to Master/mistress

8.) Do not cause permanent damage his/her submissive/slave

9.) To grow together with his/her submissive/slave

10.) Most important to do no harm his/her submissive/slave

I realize that some of these may be the same however they are not.

Essay 29 Understanding Spiritually

I was born in an Italian Catholic home. I am the only member of my family to be asked to leave Catholic School. It would seem the only class I did well it was religion. Funny I was not a stupid child I excelled on my tests when I had the will to do them. Even the ruler across the palms could not motivate me to finish my math test.

I come from a family that split in the late 60's. In 1970, I went to live with my aunt in West Virginia. She was what people would refer to as a holy roller (genuinely). The religious label was Pentecostal Holiness. Needless to say, this would have a profound effect on my thinking for the rest of my life. I joined the church went to Bible School and in 1978 I was granted papers. I understood the ritual that is a religion I had no clue about spiritually.

In 1980, I walked away from it all to discover a world I had heard was evil and bad only to find great pleasure. I was angry because I missed all the rights of passage that young people experience. The 80s where an enlightening time for me by mid-80s I found myself a single dad with a drug-addicted partner.

At the end of 1992, I found myself empty and depressed. So, depressed I thought about ending it all. (I even tried) Then I met some religious people that talked me into re-exploring the void I knew as Christianity. So, I tried. But I could not deal with the hypocrisy in them and in me. Too many things, I just could not understand or believe.

An example was in the fall of 1994 I had a legal problem with my x. I was attending a church where the pastor and several members were lawyers. I went to the Pastor for help and was set away feeling like I had done something wrong because I asked for help.

In May of 1995 life changed. I was sick and tired of being sick and tired and that is when I discovered the 12 steps. In 1996, I discovered the spiritual road known as Zen. I became a student of this idea. Since then I have come to realize that religion is the following of dogma and ritual. Being spiritual has to come within.

Some ideas I found common in most religions Spiritual laws. Laws like the law of giving. This law is a paradox. The simple version of this law is the act of giving away what you have allows you to keep it. It should be a willingness to give away the knowledge that you have to achieve more. It works really well in programs like AA for example.

In religion, the law can be taken to the extreme. Extreme? Yes, one would be expected to take a vow of poverty giving all he has to the religion.

Another law that exists is what Buddhist and Hinduism is the law of Karma. The early Christian writer Paul called this reaping what we sow.

As humans, we are complex creatures. We have a physical being, a mental being or mind and we are of a plain known as the spiritual. All religions see this and try to provide a way to find it. However, the spirit was never lost. It is with us all the time we are born with it, just as our mind and body are with us. Like our minds and body, the spirit must be fed and nurtured. For each one of us, the spirit needs differ.

To feed the body food is required, to feed the mind learning, for the spirit it is meditation. The body requires balance in its diet. The mind requires rest from the conscience, but the spirit requires fellowship. This fellowship is a connection with another human. What will make the body strong? All of its parts must work in harmony. With the mental strength comes when the mind is open to knowledge. With the spirit, it is fellowship and mediation that will give growth and strength.

Meditation is not the act of asking like in prayer. However, it is the act of listening. Listening to the inner voice and drawing strength from the powers that are all around us. It may require a mantra or chant, or it could be just drifting into pure thought. The key is to focus on the moment or just being.

Spiritually transcends the religious world. Like a young seed, it may have to die before becoming born. Like a bulb, it may sleep until the right soil comes along to cause growth. Religion may be the need soil then again religion may be what will kill the spiritual.

Unlike religion, which seeks to conquer the spirit, becoming spiritual, will come as natural as sleeping. Like a great mystery, there are clues to finding the path this is a path only you can walk. One of the paradoxes of this path is we never walk it alone. The path may seem vast but it is small.

Spiritually is like a small seed that can grow into a large tree. It needs to be nurtured and fed. And like a seed in a pot the bigger the pot the bigger the plant.

When I first started the spiritual path, I was told religion was humans search for god. And spiritually was god's search for humans. I have come to believe that is not true. Yes, religion may be the human's search for a god. But I think religion is a vehicle to the spiritual, thus spiritually is the connection with a power greater than just ourselves. If someone calls that power god then they do. What is important is the connection. Our spirit will bring out that connection and the title is not important.

So spiritually is the connection to a path. This path will lead us to a better way.

One last thought in closing. Spiritually is a part of our being, find it nurture it and allow it to grow.

Essay 30 Is it fun for you?

Is this fun for you? Is BDSM something you enjoy? Is there joy in submission? Should there be? If it is a struggle or you are not happy then you may be doing something wrong. Are you happy? Would you like to be?

Is this Fun? I was at a munch this week and a Dominant friend asked me why I canceled the classes in my home. I proceeded to explain how I did not want the politics of B/s in my home. I talked about the Zephyrhills munch and the B/s I had with MAsT: Gulf Coast.

His response was yes if it is not fun, you should not do it. I realized when I started over 20 years ago I had fun.

Then I ran into a friend who I have not seen in over a year, and he asked the same question. What happened to the NLA group I was trying to start in this area? I went into the same explanation he had the same response. If it not fun then, why do it?

Most of us choose a job or career because it is something we enjoy. There are a few who may choose a career because it is something some else may what or we are following in the footsteps of a parent or mentor (nothing wrong with that). Nevertheless, in the end, we may not be happy.

So how many times in our BDSM lives do we choose something not because we enjoy it but because we feel it is something, we must?

I think to survive in this lifestyle it is important to be happy with our selves. We should feel comfortable in our skins. This does not mean we should be free of self-doubt but it does mean we should have a basic idea of who and what we are. While others may judge us, we should only assess ourselves by our own standards. This means we may consider what others may think about us but what is more important is what we think of ourselves.

Over ten years ago, I learned a neat trick. I could shave without looking in the mirror. I did not like the face looking back at me. I had been places and done things I was not happy about. My ability to choose was compromised by one thing and when that one thing called I obeyed. The person in the mirror was not my friend and I hated him. Therefore, I was on a mission to destroy him.

Then I made a choice to end the way I was living. I found help in the rooms of the friends of Bill W and Dr. Bob and the 12 steps. This started 10 years ago in May 1995 and is not over. I look back and I made some mistakes and some poor decisions, I have made and lost friends. However, I do not regret the journey I am on.

I think it is important to discover one's self. Even if that discovery is not something others think is good. Ever since the onset of puberty, my fantasies were that of Bondage and all that goes with it. However, for years close friends have told me those "Kinky Thoughts" were evil and wrong. As a confused young man, I lacked guidance. After a career change in 1980, I started to explore life and all that had been forbidden in the past by religious dogma. In 1982, I discovered the Fantasy was real and with joy, I pursued the reality of it. With a wide-eyed innocence, I placed myself in dangers that with proper education could have been easily avoided. Then in 1987, I found that guidance.

We will make choices and we will make mistakes and we will do things right. The bottom line is this we should find happiness and joy in what we do. Whether we be Dominant, submissive or switch it is not what others may think that is important it is what we think of ourselves. We have a right to be happy and enjoy what we do. Even a slave has the right to happiness and contentment.

Essay 31 Marriage Vs Collar

Disclaimer #1:

I am not an expert on relationships I don't pretend to be. Some of the things I am planning to suggest are suggestions that have been passed on to me. Also, some of the suggestions I have tried and did not work for me may work for you.

Disclaimer #2

I am planning to make references to Biblical Dogma please remember I am not religious at one time I was & held papers in a church. But Bible School was a long time ago in a galaxy far, far away.

Disclaimer # 3:

I mean absolutely no DISRESPECT to anyone Dominant or submissive/slave or their practice of this way of life.

(Feel like the movie Dogma?)

Please note Master is non-gender and slave includes all subs, bois etc.

Marriage vs. the Collar:

Sometimes people forget a marriage is for life. I see both Master & slaves write "oh my collar is a lifetime commitment." And there is nothing wrong with that. But we seem to forget that so is a marriage. I know I have made that commitment 3 times. Was I wrong those 3 times? Looking back? I don't know! I can confess I know where I went wrong. Did I learn from my mistakes? Yes! Will I do it again? Get married? I don't know.

So here is one thing a Collar & Marriage have in common. Both are meant to be lifetime commitments.

The next thing marriage & the collar should not be entered lightly. In the time that Jesus of Nazareth walked the earth if a woman betrothed to a man, she would go to live with him in his home in a non-sexual way for a time before marriage. There were many reasons for this arrangement but the main one according to one of my Bible professors was to see if they were well matched. If they were not then the engagement could be called off with no dishonor to either party. This is the purpose of the collar of consideration time to learn about each other. What cheapens both marriage & the collar is the fact that people can meet on a Friday and are married my Monday. In the M/s D/s world, it happens all the time. Hell, I have been guilty of it. I met my third wife on a Friday and we were planning a June wedding by Sunday.

Was this a mistake? I don't know? Would I do it again? I think not but the one thing I have learned about life is never saying "never".

A long time ago a marriage was considered a contract. The collar is also considered a contract. A marriage takes work in both parts, as does a collar and please excuse the bluntness but any Master who thinks being a Master is sitting back and just give the slave orders needs to wake up. A collar like a marriage should take 100% work in both parts. And if you are reading this thinking this is B.S & my slave is my property like my "car". Well, Masters if your slave is property like your "car"? What happens when you don't take care of your car? (Point one for me). One thing I have learned about being a submissive is I may be good at taking care of other's needs but I NEED Mistress to watch out for my needs & me. I feel sometimes we forget the E in TPE.

A collar can be easily removed. A slave always has the right to ask for release! I'm sorry if that slaps some in the face and their practice of M/s relationships. But the truth is in the world of SSC or RACK if a slave asks for release, the slave should get released. My suggestion is if a Dominant says different RUN!

Now in the world of marriage, this is not so easily done. That is why there are so many divorce lawyers. Sometimes I think those of us in this way of life should have a court too (Just a Joke).

So, a marriage and a collar are not so different? It just depends on your point of view. Some people in the way of life hold the collar to a higher standard than a marriage and that is ok. Some hold a collar more special than a marriage and that is ok too. But the lesson here is the "Collar" can be cheapened the same way the "Marriage" has been over the years.

Next, let's talk about the marriage contract and the D/s contract. The D/s contract was brought into this by o as a different question but I believe it can be brought into this as well. As many of us who have been married in the past, you may not realize marriage is a contract until the judge in court awards her/him the gold mine and you get the shaft.

Yes, all agree that the D/s contract is not worth the paper it is written on. However much like a lock keeps the honest person honest.

The D/s contract keeps the honorable Master honorable when a relationship ends. It is a great commutation tool and outline for the M/s relationship. When I wrote the contract between Sir Jim and d it was written as a communication tool. Now here is something many did not know and I know Sir Jim & d do not mind me spilling the beans. They never signed the damn thing. And the reason they did not sign it was I kept forgetting to bring it. But I will say this Both Sir Jim & d have proven to be people of honor because they both have kept the spirit of the contract and the rules they have set forth for each other. So Dominants are you afraid to put your word in writing? Sir Jim like a great many other Dominants I am proud to know is a Dominant of his word. A Dominant's word is his or her bond.

Next homework I believe is Gosophor Park. The movie was ok. I will make no comments. About the movie itself. However, when looking at the interactions between the classes we should note a few things. First, those in the servant class have been trained from an early age or birth to be in that class. This included the head of the servant class. Some of the servant class were a third or fourth generation. Most of us come into this way of life at different ages. We also train or are trained differently. We understand we are willing not necessarily born or bred into a life of slavery. Some marveled at the precision of service. This is possible by practice. Much like the old joke how do you get to Carnegie Hall? Answer? Practice, practice, practice!!! Also, the Master should note if you wish that of the type of service then you invest in that type of training for your slave.

Next, the question was asked was about slavery of our world vs. slavery of the southern Antebellum (pre-civil war) or that of ancient Egypt. I don't know if I would make the comparison I don't think of myself as a slave. And I am a firm believer in the levels of submission but I don't see the slaves of Antebellum as being dishonored today by willing slaves. They were non-consensual slaves.

Slavery & submission is a paradox. A slave or sub doesn't feel free unless in service. Some have said that their slavery sets them free. And I understand the mindset, the "zone" or headspace. Remember the battle cry of the lifestyle! "To thy ownself be true!"

What I do believe dishonors the willing slavery are those who claim to be "slave" and are not. (I am not pointing to any one person or persons on this list or any other list. It is a blanket statement. I claim to be submissive. But there are those who either to my face or behind my back said I am no submissive. People have said, "Paul is just another confused person". And by some standards, I may never be a "true" submissive. But I do not go by others standards I go by what pleases Mistress & what is in my heart.")

Which brings me to the question of surrender and the question of love. To me, surrender & love go hand in hand. Am I saying you can't surrender unless you are in love? No. Some practice what I would call "Mr. Spock" D/s or D/s without emotions. And it is possible for some to suppress their emotions well, while others cannot.

I believe total surrender comes with trust. This trust a Master should be willing to earn. I'm sorry I have been burned too many times by the words "trust me". I have learned that trust is as precious as honor, loyalty, and honesty. Qualities Both Master & slave should have. Once the lines of trust have been established then surrender can come. And surrender is not waving the white flag but surrender in this way of life is also a paradox. Nether is surrender giving up. But it is a letting go. To me what makes this surrender easily is love. (Passing out barf bags). I think with your level of surrender comes your level of submission for example before Mistress & I formed our little-blended family the issue of money was kept separate. As we grew in love we grow in trust with the level of trust brings on a deeper level of surrender & with the deeper level of surrender brings the deeper level of submission.

One thing I have learned in the last few years if you build a relationship with a good foundation then the relationship should stand. I also I have learned that anything worth having is worth working for. And anything easily gained is not appreciated.

Essay 32 My First time

It was sometime in 1982 I had left the church 2 years before over the SM issues. It had always been a fantasy. I had the BDSM porno magazines and newspapers. I read the personal ads and thought about contacting someone in the ad. But I did not know where to start or what to say. I was so green. I was working in north New Jersey. I had done a bondage fantasy with my wife and she hated it. So, I was left with my collection.

I read an ad for a place called Club O, in NYC. I finally go up the courage to answer the ad. It was a Friday night and I found myself taking a cab from Penn station over to the club. I should note I drank a lot back then when I left the church I was making up for lost time. I partied hard. Anyway, that night I decided to attend sober. Good choice too. I stood at the bottom of the stairs I paid my $25 and went up. There was a female couple doing breast bondage. I must admit it was the first time I saw anything like that live. Oh, I've seen plenty of SM 8mm films but never anything that close or real. I sat next to two ladies. Both dressed very nice and both very Dominant. The ladies were very friendly. Did one ask me was I a Dominant or a submissive? Hell, if I knew. All I knew at that point was this is real. So, I answered Dominant I think. I did not know. She leaned over and said, "if you want to be a good Dominant you must learn to be a good submissive" Later I would learn this type of training was called "from the Bottom-up".

So, it started my journey. I took off my clothing and sat at her feet naked as her ashtray. Smoking was allowed back then. I could not believe myself. But I was like a sponge to this teacher. I also was invited home with the female couple that night but I declined. I said no out of fear. Something I would regret later.

This is the story of my first time. It has been a wonders journey. Not always fun. But I don't regret the 34 years. And I look forward to doing this well into my 80s.

Essay 33 A letter to a new Dominant

A letter to a new Dominant

Introduction:

Last night I was talking with a new Dominant about our lifestyle. This morning while having my coffee I have composed this letter. I like the contents of this letter so I plan to share it with you. I have removed all personal references. I hope this enlightens new people on our lists.

A letter to a new Dominant

I have given a lot of thought to our conversation last night. As I sit here with my morning coffee, I think about all the wonderful things you are about to learn. Some of the things that are taken for granted by some of us. The new terms you will learn RACK, SSC, Power Exchange, BDSM, and D/s. You are entering a world that is diverse and yet grounded in principles. Principles of honor, respect, and trust. This is a world of consent. Consent is the cornerstone of everything we do. This lifestyle has a diverse sub-culture, sub-cultures like the Old Guard, Leather, Gor, and the Victorian. People will refer to themselves as Dominant, submissive, switch, top or bottom.

First, let us talk about The Power Exchange.

The submissive has the power and it is surrender to you. She/he must willingly surrender it as "a gift" (for lack of a better word). A true dominant doesn't take the submission. But receives it. Because a person is a submissive does not mean she/he is your submissive. I believe both a Dominant & submissive should treat each other with a certain amount of common courtesy. But you will meet those who feel this is not necessary. Keep in mind that the submissive is a person first with feelings & ideas. The gift of submission can be revoked at any time. And when this "gift" is taken back you need to learn to let it go. And for some letting go is not an easy task. As the submissive surrenders, the power to you it will be your job to direct that power and manage it. It takes a great amount of trust on the part of the submissive to surrender power. It takes honor & respect on our part to direct it.

Trust

The trust factor is a major part of the power exchange. If the submissive does not trust you she/he will not surrender that power. You should never assume that trust is yours on demand. Trust is something you must be willing to earn. And I will admonish you; if you violate trust it will be very hard to earn it back if you can ever earn it back. You will make mistakes in the matter of trust. My advice is simple. Own up to your mistakes, and learn from them. You will hurt people in your journey. You must try to make amends when you do hurt someone. If you are unable to make amends then simply clean your side of the street. People will also hurt either knowingly or unknowingly. Again, I would advise you to do what is necessary to move on.

Some submissives expect the Dominant to be flawless. They expect us to be more than human. Just be yourself. There is a code of honor we should live by and some of us do for others this is just a game. A role they play at night in the bedroom and that is ok. For others, this is a 24/7 lifestyle and that is ok too. Some will use you just for the casual sex part of this lifestyle. It is your choice to be used or not. Remember there is always a choice. Just respect someone else's choice.

To start your journey, I would suggest you buy the book "The Loving Dominant". I want you to attend the local munches and seminars. If you are invited to a play party go watch another dominant work. Ask questions. Make friends.

Essay 34 Questions asked by a submissive

Dear Sir Paul

I have a question...when meeting a Dom for the first time, is it reasonable that he should accept my limits??

My Answer

The answer is yes, he should not only should he accept them he should respect them. I'm glad you wrote this month is going to be a little crazy. I am moving and trying to pack and get my kid to realize he is on his own.

This is not a lecture, and I know how hard it can be being a single parent. I have been down that road and at a time when men were expected to walk away. But you must not compromise or put yourself in danger. And if some person calling himself a Dom and will not adhere to your limits then you don't need that.

You should set yourself a set of standards; I know how lonely things can get. But it is not worth selling yourself and self-respect short.

First meeting protocols

When meeting a Dominant both submissive and slave

1.) You should meet in a public place. Never accept an invitation to meet at the person's home. You would not do that if it was a vanilla meeting so why meet privately for a BDSM meeting. Munches and public dungeons are good first meeting places.

2.) Have a save call. Call some at the beginning of the meeting just to let a friend know where you are. Also, call when the meeting is over. Always put your safety first.

3.) Don't play in the first meeting. You don't know him/her and he/she doesn't know you. Get to know each other first.

4.) Avoid drinking; drinking will lower your inhabitations.

5.) Make yourself a list of what you want. D/s or BDSM is not a 50/50 relationship it is 100% both ways.

Last you may be a submissive but that doesn't mean you are submissive to all those who may call themselves Dominant.

Essay 35 Love, sex, and the Master slave relationship.

What are you looking for? Love? Try E-harmony. Is love possible within a true M/s relationship?

This is a question I have pondered many times. This is a subject with passion. Within the Master/slave relationship is love practical? I've heard it said no it isn't practical. I've heard it said it isn't necessary. Yet I've been in love many times. Some believe love gets in the way of the

Master. They believe you really can't discipline your slave if you love him/her. You can't truly punish if you are in love. And I have wondered this myself. I really don't believe that any type of punishment in a relationship can be healthy. Although I have done it in the past. But punishment is another topic which I have addressed in the past.

So, love is it healthy for a true Master/slave relationship? I don't know I've never had a relationship that did not have love as a part of it. Maybe that is the flaw in my thinking.

Which brings the next question. Can a person live without love? We all have different "Loves" in our lives. I have a son whom I love dearly. I love his wife. And I have four wonderful grandchildren whom I would die for. But family love is different than the love I'm talking about.

Does love have to be sexual? I believe not. Yes, sex can be an expression of love. But humans have the ability to be sexual without love. I know I have done it many times in my past. Does an M/s relationship have to have a sexual component? No, but it can benefit a relationship, just as BDSM play doesn't have to be a component in a Master/slave relationship. However, there are benefits to BDSM play.

Relationships are complex, needing honesty, communication, and trust. And in an M/s relationship consent. Love, sex, and BDSM are the added complexity of the components to M/s. But the question is are they essential to a relationship. My answer is I don't know. I need love in my life, I crave SM play, and as I get older I am not as sexual as I once was but still would love it.

Essay 36 The Differences Between BDSM and Abuse

A Guide for People Involved in Consensual and Non-Consensual BDSM Activities

BDSM is an acronym for "Bondage, Discipline, Sadomasochism," terms used by the alternative sexuality community for activities such as Dominance and submission (consensual power play) and other role-playing games, tying up a partner, spanking, flogging, and a variety of other mutually satisfying, CONSENSUAL activities. BDSM is not abuse.

Often, BDSM is confused with abuse due to the very nature of its activities.

However, the differences, as you will see below, are very profound. BDSM activities are ALWAYS Safe, Sane and

Consensual.

Abuse is NEVER safe, NEVER sane, and NEVER

Consensual.

BDSM follows established rules. Abuse has no rules.

BDSM is always negotiated for the safety of both partners.

Abuse is not negotiated.

BDSM activities are used for mutual pleasure. Abuse holds pleasure only for the abuser.

In BDSM, the submissive partner uses a 'safe word' to stop any activity they do not wish to engage in.

During an Abusive activity, the victim cannot stop what is happening to them.

BDSM activities are not intended to physically or emotionally injure a partner.

Abusers want to hurt their partners physically, emotionally, or both.

BDSM is a loving form of sexual expression. Abuse is a crime of power and control.

BDSM involves 'aftercare' - hugging, cuddling, and caring.

Abuse involves 'aftercare' for bruises, cuts, broken bones, and emotional terror.

BDSM activities NEVER take place in front of children or other family members

Abuse often happens in front of children, family members, and friends.

Practitioners of BDSM never participate in activities while under the influence of drugs or alcohol.

Abuse often occurs when the abuser has been using drugs or alcohol.

In BDSM, the partners involved give up power voluntarily and temporarily, but ALWAYS maintain their individual rights.

In Abusive relationships, the abuser takes away any rights the victim may have.

Anyone who forces you to participate in BDSM activities against your will IS NOT practicing BDSM!

They are engaging in abuse and/or rape.

Essay 37 Communication

In any relationship, good communication is an important factor. In BDSM the cornerstone of a relationship is consent. Another foundation stone is trust. With trust and consent comes communication.

Communication defined as a noun

1. the act or process of communicating; the fact of being communicated.

2.the imparting or interchange of thoughts, opinions, or information by speech, writing, or signs.

3.something imparted, interchanged, or transmitted.

4. a document or message imparting news, views, information, etc.

5. passage, or an opportunity or means of passage, between places.

6. communications. means of sending messages, orders, etc., including telephone, telegraph, radio, and television. routes and transportation for moving troops and supplies from a base to an area of operations.

7. Biology. activity by one organism that changes or has the potential to change the behavior of other organisms. transfer of information from one cell or molecule to another, as by chemical or electrical signals.

Not only do you need to communicate. It needs to be honest, open and often. It needs to be an important factor as important as trust and consent. It should work both ways. Simply saying "I'm the master do as I say" isn't good enough. I submissive and slave have the right to ask questions. Questions should be asked respectfully. And as Master, you have a responsibility to answer those questions. And sometimes you will need to explain yourself.

Master/slave or Dominant/submissive relationships are complex. And good communication is the key to a healthy relationship. And a healthy relationship will last. If your relationship doesn't last communication might be the key.

There are different methods of communication. You can keep a journal. For those in M/s or D/s relationships try the "the slave journal". The submissive/slave writes open honest feeling without the worry or repercussion.

Have time out. That is when you step out of the rolls of Master/slave or Dominant/submissive and talk on a human level.

Final thought, communication, trust, and consent make for a good foundation to any relationship whether it is based in BDSM or just a vanilla relationship. Relationships take work. But they are worth it.

Final thoughts:

I've seen a lot in my life. In my life as a Leather Master, I've seen a lot of abuse done in the name of this. Once I decided to play submissive to this female dominant. I thought she was ok and I was young and lack experience. No one told me about Negotiation or safety. And I thought this would be BDSM training. You see good masters start out training as submissives. But instead, I did work around the house and some house cleaning for 2 days. At the end of the second day, she did some BDSM play. She used a hood which made me extremely uncomfortable and I could not enjoy myself.in the end, she stole $90 out of my wallet and called it tribute. Had I been properly educated that weekend would have never happened.

I write to educate people. I feel education is the most important part of the BDSM lifestyle. Not just for submissive and slaves but for dominants and masters. Mistakes can happen and no one person is perfect. However, I believe a lot of "stuff" that happens can be avoided with a good education.

I am no longer active in this but I stay in touch with what is going on. I write for the benefit of others. I want you to understand this really isn't safe. There are predators, abusers and people looking to cheat involved in this. Safety is most important and the best way to stay safe is to be educated. Look out for yourself, have fun and avoid all the traps. In the 34 years, I've been doing this I've had lots of fun, and I have lived out fantasies. If you do educate yourself, you will have fun too.